D0776855

A Schedule of Benefits

John N. Morris

A Schedule of Benefits

ATHENEUM NEW YORK

1987

Certain of these poems first appeared in print as follows:
GRAND STREET, *Visiting the Province, Untrimming the Tree*, Hamlet *at Sea, His Will, Flying Lessons, The Turing Game, The Club of the Only Children*
THE NEW REPUBLIC, *Steichen at Art*
THE NEW YORKER, *Bringing Up Father, The Old Hand, The Country Beyond the Hill*
PERSPECTIVE, *Our Daily Visitor, 911*
POETRY, *Reading the Writing, Grandfather's Picture, The Grand Birthday, A Schedule of Benefits, The Museum Shop Catalogue, The Cure, Boxtrap, A Word from the Examiners, Reading Myself Asleep*
THE SEATTLE REVIEW, *A Particular Child, The Visiting Hours*
THE SEWANEE REVIEW, *The Disappearance of Sideshows, The Parson's Tale, The Alterations, The Unburied*
THE YALE REVIEW, *In the Album*
The dedicatory poem I reprint from an earlier book, *The Life Beside This One* (1975). J.N.M.

ATHENEUM
Macmillan Publishing Company
866 Third Avenue, New York, N.Y. 10022
Collier Macmillan Canada, Inc.

Library of Congress Cataloging-in-Publication Data

Morris, John N.
    A schedule of benefits.

    I. Title.
PS3563.08744S34   1987   811'.54   87-23441
ISBN 0-689-11950-X (pbk.)
ISBN 0-689-11949-6 (hc.)

Designed by Harry Ford

10 9 8 7 6 5 4 3 2 1

Printed in the United States of America

FOR MY MOTHER IN THE WOODS

Charlotte Marshall Maurice Hammond
1909–1986

In the story I tell
We are still sitting there
In that story her childhood
That she is unfolding about her
While the surprising
Water falls through the woods
Out of the hill under her mother's garden.

Here we have walked through the woods
Where she walked with her mother,
And the water is falling exactly where they found it,
And I sit on the stone where she sat
Before I was there, before her childhood
Turned into the world where I sit
In her marvellous story.

I am sitting there now
In the story I tell
In the place I shall never revisit,
I with my mother and she
Perhaps with hers;
And the stone is there;
And the water is there as it was,
And still it is going away and is not returning.

I

I I

I I I

I

READING THE WRITING

With his own hand he has given himself away.
"You are very secretive and fearful," she says
For twenty dollars, his mail-order explainer.
"You show no generosity to people
Or to yourself. Try not to be deceitful."
This is not palmistry. What she has read
Is something he has written.
Like everyone else he is a man of letters.

He thinks what she has read was written
Decades ago when first he was forming
His characters after the various models
His hand in its cunning
Always succeeded in failing
To be more than a variation on.
Only the *J* of his John Hancock is John Hancock's.
So he became himself, like everyone.

She has taught him a lesson, his accuser.
All this he had hidden in the open,
Showing everyone no generosity to himself.
Perhaps in the future he will send
Himself only to the printer, who will reform him.
For now, he is trying not to be deceitful.
He is giving himself away. Here. In his own hand.

THE PERIOD ROOMS

In the West Wing we house
What we have left of houses,
What we have fetched from destruction.
Taking an educated care

Coolly the curators own them for us—
Interiors they forbid us to enter,
One somewhere after another set aside
For us casually to inspect.

Till now they have chosen chiefly to exhibit
Colonial near-emptiness and, jam-packed
With comfort, the mahogany and rosewood
Public rooms of the plush Victorian rich

Where, unimaginably like us, someone
After someone lived in hope and stepped
A last time from the door we glance through
And closed it in our unforeseeable faces.

Delicate curatorial saws have saved
These appearances, these lustres. The verifying
Dust revised away, on these walls
They hang these walls, a show of pictures

Of what was once someone's intention
About the future. One imagines
In a clarifying weather sawyers and joiners
Whistling about their exemplary work

A thousand miles away. In that elsewhere
A set of coordinates hangs in the air,
The bare Idea of it. In the West Wing
We observe its wooden imitation.

And in the basement are folded away
Other interior spaces. The curators prepare
A change of exhibit. Out of their packing cases
As if from nowhere for our edification

What walls may not arise, what scene
Stiff with the furnishings of recollection
May not expose itself to view?
Large as the life that may not enter there,

The black armoire, the Spanish chest and the appalled
Four-poster and the tingling clock are here
In curatorial detail restored,
Never again to be at last forgotten.

GRANDFATHER'S PICTURE

Under an uncertain
Mountain the slate lake
Tips from the pictureboard,
Skews in the forest frame. Wind
Troubles the amateur water.
Who but Grandfather's survivors
Could know where they are in his only painting
In these woods in the 1880's
In the unskillful Adirondacks?

Yet something here is accomplished. An effect
Is obtained. Already it is there
In the 1880's—the Ghost, our guideboat
And family cult. So delicate is it, it exists
To be taken care of. Here our purpose is
That it survive us, that it shall remain.

In this picture it waits to receive me
Into the family in the 1930's,
This hard speck
Dead white a hundred years ago in the water.
And there is the cottage. Under that paint
Where I sit, perhaps one of the girls—
Marian, Margaret, Emily, Cornelia Joline—
Just now finishes reading
This mint copy of Bellamy's *Looking Backward.*
The idea is, never to change.

They came by train and buckboard
To the distant summer. Only the rich
Would choose so much simplicity. They drove
Their own cow to it, her bag
Swagging through the Adirondacks.

In the photograph someone has not taken yet,
Sisters and brothers they stand before me.
They line the porch railing. They are plain
As our family nose on their faces.
They have their backs to the water.
They do not know this is the last century.

This morning from the perfect water
Arises a cool steam.
Were I to step to the window
In Grandfather's picture
Perhaps I should see him
Regarding these diamond panes
He here distantly recorded.
As hard as paint can make it
In the corner of my eye he is keeping
The Ghost in trust for the children.
So delicate is it, it survives us.
This is the last century.
A preserved wind blows through it.
The idea is, never to change.

THE GRAND BIRTHDAY

To the grand birthday
As to funeral, wedding or christening,
Summoned, we come. From our houses
We hurry home,
Antaeus touching down.
All weekend our cars
Loll on the lawn in a litter of color.
What assemble here are
So many departures.
We are bound by
What we diverge from—
The Source in his frame,
The pattern of our features.

Our flesh and blood,
We are meat and drink to us.
We refresh us.
Deep in our silver cups
In stories like mirrors
We repeat ourselves.
The past is real,
That ferocious whiskey.
This is where we were
When we were becoming.
We live in our relations.

Outside our circle
Our wives, our husbands
Look on us in some wonder.
They believed we were who we are,
Not this hurry of semblance,
These unlikely tales in variorum.
Till Sunday they withdraw from us.
But in our images the children
Are mastering every story.
They are learning how to repeat us.
They are establishing a text.

By Sunday we are all tired of us.
(*While there is death*
There's hope, perhaps we say.)
From the grand birthday
As from altar or font or graveside,
In our brilliant ovens we steer away
Into our other places.
                          Beside us
The children are growing their faces.
Though they will depart from us,
Though they will corrupt the text,
They are inheriting us.
The Source is in his frame.
We are born again.
They are who we were.
We smile at our executors.

IN OUR ELEGIES

Our Father who art in Heaven—insubordinate
That clause telling him where he is.
Give us this day our daily bread.
On our knees we issue our instructions.
In detail we tell him what we believe
About his family and then we eat one of him.
Our mouths are full of what we desire.

As in our elegies. The dead we call by name.
We tell them who they are and where they died
On what occasion. As if they had forgotten.
We tell them why we invoke them.
As if they were somewhere still they remind us
A little of our lives—almost the only ones
We still almost believe in.
As if the words themselves were mercy,
That daily bread,
While we are somewhere still
With our breath they inform us.
They fill us full of our desiring.

VISITING THE PROVINCE

Generations ago this is somewhere
I come from, a place I have gone
Looking for. Over the faithful
Villages the Union Jacks
Snap in the Atlantic
Wind. This morning my son
Killed his first fish.
It lies in his gut, its
Shadow in my camera.
This is our innocent
Last day in the Province.

This is only somewhere we come from
Generations ago. Who, then,
Suddenly do these soldiers
Dressed as the leaves that cover the ground
Think we are
In their checkpoint on the motorway?
But these rifles are a touch
Of the authentic! I am afraid
I am thrilled to be taken
For dangerous at gunpoint.

In fact, they rightly suspect us
Of nothing. But this morning
A boy of eleven, my son's age,
Lost his hand in Belfast
Where no one will find it.
Though we are a boring
Work, thank God!—will not
Blow up in their English faces—
They dowse in our luggage.
Inch by inch the sergeant
Admires the hired car. So intent
Is he I fear

For a moment he will find it,
Whatever it is.
                    He smiles. He suggests
We have a pleasant journey. And waves us on.

They are going to keep on searching
For years until they never find it
Again, what they are looking for.
Near the border we will be taken
Apart once more, cautious hands
Deploring the foreign laundry.
Though we resume our pleasant journey,
Though we put them behind us
Dressed as the leaves that cover the ground,
They do not disappear into the landscape.
A catch is in the creel.
These images I carry home.
Touring the picturebook
Republic I remember
Something a little like the real,
That famous explosive.
Perhaps that is where I come from.
All night I slip back over the border.
I am ashamed. I am thrilled.
Whatever it is,
This time perhaps we shall find it.

UNDER SIX FLAGS

Once upon one time or another
This seems to have been almost everywhere,
Even France before the Revolution.
Now flag after flag tells us
Where we are not any longer.
That is the theme of the park.
We have passed through several states
To achieve this destination.
Now we know where we haven't arrived.
This is the middle of America.

And bound to be terribly expensive.
Though inside everything is free
Except the necessities,
I once bought a car for less
Than entry here for five will cost me.
Still, we came to have the nice day
Everyone has been wishing on us,
And so I charge it up against the card,
Promising to pay for all this innocence later.

This is the garden of falling.
Beyond the turnstile the children
Break toward a screaming
As of whole high schools of the drawn-and-quartered.
They tear away from us to join them
On the railroad above the trees
Hurtling through some principles of topology.
They are here to fear for their lives in safety.
Patiently they wait in line impatiently
Over and over again
For the bottom to drop out of something.

Their mother and father no longer
Incline to these excitations. We wander
Off among the rest of us
Easy targets (why are so many of us

So fat? why do so many caps
Sell us poisons or fertilizer?).
First we raft the Colorado for a minute,
Then take the gasoline
Powered streamtrain through the Bayou Country.
There is nothing to do between the thrills
Except eat a ten-inch Footlong Hotdog
In the Old English beerless Mexican cantina.
All day we will all be good
As in the oldest of regimes,
Pasturing here under the screaming trees,
Browsing like the beasts that perish.

For hours I take my pleasure like a man.
By four I have had my nice day at last.
Even the children are tired
Of falling over and over.
They have not died a dozen times
And that is enough for one summer.
Now it is time we were exchanging
This place where everything
Is almost exactly like something
For home where nothing is quite as it seems.
As the rule is, we exit at the entrance.
Over the black plaza we carry
Our exhaustion to the car.
Though we have been nowhere together
Everything was worth all of the money.
We came here to have nothing happen
To us for a day. And were not disappointed.
This was this time and not another.
Now miles of how we arrived here lie before me.
Thousands of people are screaming.
We strap ourselves into our own machine.

A TRAVELLERS' ADVISORY

for a son, newly licensed

Now the danger you are in must protect you.
Knowing how hundreds of sharp pounds
Per square inch of possible implosion
Surround you, for the first few inexpert
Thousands of miles you will be careful.
But soon you will have mastered
This congeries of the Simple Machines
Working to your mechanical advantage.
A finger steers these tons,
This polished box of velocity.
Your learned nerves and habitual
Small muscles preserve you.
For a time you may confide in your skill.
Now you are free to get somewhere in a hurry.
Every day you escape by thoughtless inches.

In these things we did not trust
Me to instruct you.
For fear I should harm us we hired it done.
So it does not become me to warn you
Against the last finger of whiskey—
One for the road, that *viaticum.*
Still, though we can hardly bear it
That I should have anything to teach you,
A Travellers' Advisory is out.
On the High Plains a wind is rising
Into which you have been loosed.
Though the car fill with your enlarging children,
Most of these miles you must drive alone.
From this no belt or pillow of air
Nor any skill can protect you.
Though all the purposes cross
And the maps are out of date
And the signs point in every direction,
Into what is hurrying at you,
Dear boy, steer better than your father.

IN THE ALBUM

In moments we appeared,
In sixty seconds blossoming on the paper.
Brilliantly we are there, this whole bookful of us
With not a thought in our paper heads.
And everywhere we are smiling. Always
The idea seems to be to turn our backs on
Something tremendous—the South Rim, say,
Or Niagara ruining behind us.

Now we all stare with my stare.
For I am here chiefly as the point of view—
Invisible but the without-which-nothing.
My business is composition, keeping
Us close together inside the hard edges
Where we pause for these moments of reflection.

Though the dyes are unstable and the manufacturer
Does not guarantee the chemistry that arrests us
And the light disappearing into the spaces
Between the pictures gives back a flat blackness,
Tonight, rightly, by lamplight we just look
At the pictures. We stare us in our faces,
Ignoring everything that lies about us.

BRINGING UP FATHER

For too long he has followed too much
The devices of his own heart.
It falls to you to restrain him.
The family is not a democracy. Rely
On instinct and your immense
Power to terrify. *Out of his exhausted sleep*
You bring him bolt-upright in a moment.
At first this discipline is almost total.

He has illusions, and you are one of them.
Every day he brings you
Himself for your approbation.
Though his belief in you is unbounded,
Tutor him in disappointment.
Like you he will have to learn
To live with your limitations. (You, too,
Must modify your expectations:
Nothing you can do
Will make him always just and kind,
Though he aches for your admiration.)

At times you will have wondered
What was in it for you. Indulge yourself.
Run screaming from the house.
For hours he will understand you.
He, too, has his despairs. Like you
He will cry out
Against the world that it has wronged him.
"The best is not to be born,"
He will say, the enormous baby!

In time you will leave him alone.
This is the school of kindness.
You say goodbye to him,

This imperfection.
You have made a life for him.
He shares your disappointment.
This is what you both embrace,
Meeting and parting. You cleave to this.
At last he will leave you
The empty nest, abandon
You to the care of your children.
At last he will have learned
Everything they have to teach you.

UNTRIMMING THE TREE

Now all that scintillation is a chore.
What they so recently assembled
Piece by piece in imitation
Of every year for twenty years ago

Each day became more everyday.
The delicate contrivances ignored,
This clutter in a corner of the eye
Now is an hour on the stepladder

And woman's work. This afternoon,
The sunlight brave and January thin
Reflecting on her, she sets down
Lightlier than they lifted them

Angel and orb and cardboard cornucopia,
The candy cane old as the eldest child.
Once she has packed away the annual farm
(Each cotton sheep plump as a thumb),

Hanging the glassy surface of the lake
Up on its hook in the back bedroom,
She sends the snowy field out to the laundry.
Arms full of a great weightlessness she arises

Toward the airless year in the black attic.
The Season's Greetings flutter in the trash
Out in the alley and the tree,
Naked, imitates mere nature.

All's done but this—that at the last she blind
The windows of the Advent Calendar
From which next year again shall stare
The forest animals as day by day,

As the great Day approaches
Until the Manger stands revealed,
Husband and child and wife, restored
Out of the storm, once more shall be assembled.

II

STEICHEN AT ART

Across two pages four ensigns are disposed
Waiting to fly in fresh khakis. In brilliant gray
A level light shines from the left,
Fetched here to Florida from an Italian century.
How bored they are in the beautiful picture!
This is *Steichen at War*. The irony
Is cheap at the price: forty dollars.

The war is in the air. Here Steichen suspends
A Dauntless divebomber over Wake Island,
Pilot and gunner in profile, standing
Still at a couple of hundred miles per hour.
(That black burst of flak will never touch them.)
Or, imperfectly composed, a Japanese
Blazes before us. He burns
For forty years fifty feet from the water.

Close up, almost everyone is delighted
To be here, especially the wounded.
I find only one who detests us.
In the ready room where he prepares
Himself for tomorrow he despises
The avid eye, our relishing attention.
He stares through the dark box proposed to him.
That he hates us makes a lovely picture.

All these young men we owe to Edward Steichen
At art, who here is said to have said
Print it darker. Deeper and darker.
They have all been cropped
According to his directions.
For about a dollar a year
Here has he preserved them
To us, these apparitions.
Ask the ravishing dead: it's a bargain.

THE DISAPPEARANCE OF
SIDESHOWS

" 'The sideshows are all disappearing,' he
says. 'The Two-Faced Man is dead. His
wife, the Alligator Woman, is no longer
with us. The midget's wife is sick, so he's
not on the road. The Giant is in the hos-
pital, and the Fat Man had a heart attack.
The Elephant Lady can't walk anymore.
And Freddy the Hermaphrodite is dead.' "

Parade magazine

They disappear, these imperfections,
These images of what may be borne.
In the hospital the Giant is grieving.
How he will miss their familiar
Faces and the everyday
Marriages of the damaged!

Who would not arrange for them
Some story if he could,
A Florida of words
Where they might assemble
In caravan forever?
They do not desire it.
If only we would suffer them
To shine in our regard!
It is their gift
To be themselves
To serve us, our consolors.

Exceptions, they offer us
Themselves as fit
For our admiration. *Like us*
They do not wish to be
Like us. Although they must.
The sideshows are all disappearing.
In the hospital lies a great grieving
In the image of what must be borne.

HAMLET AT SEA

> "I invited Captain Hawkins to a fishe din-
> ner and had *Hamlet* acted abord me, which
> I permitt to keepe my people from idle-
> nesse and unlawful games, or sleepe."
>
> *From the log of Captain William
> Keeling, Master of the* Dragon, *in
> convoy to the East Indies, 1607.*

Now the sun has gone to the Americas.
By pinnace Captain Hawkins comes
Across an evening in the South Atlantic
To the *Dragon* for this entertainment:
Fish first; then *Hamlet*.
As if they were part of the play
In important chairs handled out of the cabin
The captains sit like Claudius and Gertrude
Not twenty feet from Denmark.

What they will be shown from the fo'c'sle
Will not be, as at first may appear,
Just a long joke about watchstanding
As that is misunderstood in the army.
But the Globe *is* half the world away.
This is *Hamlet* at sea: in these latitudes
Some latitude must be granted.
For weeks while they have been
Clambering down Africa the cast has rehearsed it.
Now all that havering about being—
Even the groundlings up in the shrouds
Know it by heart and join in,
Rogues and peasant slaves in chorus.
Ophelia is acted by the ship's boy
To much witty play upon her name.
And the Bosun, being so majestical,
Is the Ghost. When that fellow in the cellarage
Below decks commands serious hearing,

Everyone almost falls into the sea laughing.
And all cheer their hero
The decisive Dane when they hear how

He impetuously boarded the pirate
Leaving to his companions
As sealed orders his avenging will.
At the end when everyone who dies
Does so broadly, even the captains are smiling.

This is 1607. No one wonders what it means.
A half mile into the darkness
One of us the uninvited,
Standing his watch on Captain Hawkins' ship,
Cannot make out that far-off palaver.
But he wishes he had some part in it.
In snatches of the Good Quarto
What comes across the water is merriment.

Over all this the Master of the *Dragon* presides.
For pity of us and for our discipline
He permits it,
The lawful game that holds us from our sleep.
It sounds like happiness at a distance.

THE SILVER HAND

The City in these pages is imaginary.
The people, the places are all fictitious.
Only the police routine is based on
established investigatory techniques.
                                    —Ed McBain

Thus the bold disclaimer: Only Art.
In lines he underlines how he denies
Terrors he has taken pains to delineate.
We must not believe in what grips us.

When I was eight all summer
I disappeared into the pen-and-ink
Howard Pyle illustrations of *Otto*
Of the Silver Hand I still inhabit.

A land is locked in those pages.
Even unread, no one will escape.
Though on the shelf, on the chemical paper
The people, the places turn to ash,

Some days, behind those lines,
A child stares from the Dragon's House
In his head across antique Germany.
He is one whom someone made believe

This is *wie es eigentlich gewesen ist*:
The wound, the silver hand, its iron grip.

THE PARSON'S TALE

The sun from the south line has steeply descended
As we slip through the chilling villages, our shadows
Twelve feet tall behind us. Unfinished,
We nevertheless draw to this conclusion.
We are going home in our common story.

Now only one story is lacking,
Though many of us have been left unspoken.
Almost fulfilled is all the ordinance.
We are all but one silent now,
Speechless in chorus.

We shall get no fable from him, he assures us.
He will knit up all this feast and make an end,
Showing us the way we have taken.
In our seven sins he arrays us.
He would save us if he could.
Now is the hour of prose
Hopeful of our emendation.

All that is written is written to our doctrine.
Though it is late for this. Now we may all disappear
Into our destination. Though our author repents him
That he has made us, publishing his Retraction,
We are not lost like the loud *Book of the Lion*.
He has saved us as he could,
Each of us one of the untold millions,
Our breathless lives bursting with their stories.

III

A SCHEDULE OF BENEFITS

It is a part of the policy.
On this paper you find
How highly they value
Those things that may happen
To you in time. Before your eyes
Your eyes are written
Down at half a million.
They will replace each hand
With fifty thousand dollars.
Piecemeal you are worth a fortune.

But perhaps nothing
Of this will happen. Then
You will never receive them,
The benefits. Certain
Exclusions, too, are written in.
If you have lost your life
Without noticing it
Somewhere in your forties
Or misplaced it perhaps in childhood,
That casualty does not appear on the schedule.

Still, for years for every month that passes
You will have your salary
By way of compensation.
Over the door of your job
Is written *Arbeit Macht Frei.*
You are assured you will get
What is coming to you.
Though this is not a part of any policy.
That finally must be your consolation.

THE OLD HAND

When at last you win to the rich coast
The Old Hands utter their glad, discouraging cry:
Too late! Thus they greeted also Odysseus.

At the very earliest you will arrive
As they are cleaning up after the Revolution,
Now only a little blood on the courtyard wall.

Not for you the authenticating squalor:
The poor they have put out of your misery,
And torture by beggary is much abated.

On the whole the real is long ago.
That was before they put in the airport.
Now nothing need detain the serious traveller.

Under glass in the rest-house bedroom
A version of your language warns you:
The Hour of Arrival is the Hour of Departure.

Press on. The far interior awaits you,
A timorous history you almost understand.
There you will dress in your native colors

Where nothing has at last detained its traveller.
As clearly as you can you warn each visitor:
Something may happen here. But not to you.

THE MUSEUM SHOP CATALOGUE

The past is perfectly darling—
These pretty things that come along with us!
Mary and Siva house without oppugnancy.
This is not the Museum
Without Walls but the Emporium.
Pages of images are exposed for sale.

We take them out of the grave
And Europe for our entertainment.
And surround them with delighted prose.
Here is "William, the unofficial
Mascot of the Museum," a hippopotamus
From some Dynasty or other.
In our own words these things belong to us.
This "amusing box" we shall
Keep nothing in comes to us
From the Oratory of San Lorenzo.
Everything here has been imported
Over some frontier. At last
It is all a kind of art entirely.

And in faithful reproduction. Never before
This century could every antique
Carelessness of hand be exactly recorded.
Even time is imitated here,
The imperfect destroyer:
As a last touch the precise shade
Of faded pigment is added.

And really they *are* just lovely,
Perfectly lovely, these things.
In vain do I deplore.
A desire fingers these pages.
Offered at a price one can afford,
They are made for us.
We dot them down on bookshelf and table.
Mary and Siva

Accompany our lives.
Although a loneliness persists.
They are only beautiful now.
In microscopic detail
They are made for us to ignore.

And here, tiny, are the great pictures
We send at Christmas with our warm regard.

HIS WILL

It has taken him his whole life
To form it. Now he deploys it.
He appoints, he directs and requires.
Never before such imperial gestures!
For once somebody else
Will have to pay his just debts.
This jargon elates him.

His will is that his will
Shall survive him. In his hand he holds
His heirs and assigns forever.
He knows what they are worth
In detail. A price is set on every head.
In the end they will learn
Exactly how much he owes them.

His every word a joy to him,
He appends the clause *in terrorem*,
Although he knows that at last
For once everyone will obey him.
In discharge of their obligation
At last they will do as he wills,
Burying him strictly *per* their instructions.

FLYING LESSONS

Out of our sight surfaces
And smooth thousands
Of tiny explosions support him.
Yesterday he was practicing
His touch-and-go's—landing,
Taking off and landing. Difficult stuff.
Today he's back on S-turns
And straight-and-level or just stooging
Around all over the landscape.

He is looking down on us, the pattern
Where he lives. If he visited
It now this map would kill him.
In these lessons he thinks he is learning
To rise above it, put everything
In perspective. Our purposes
Unfold before him. We are driving
Home in our own dimensions.
Rushing there brings us to a standstill.

And now his hour is up and he
Too hastens to a standstill. Ears
Crackling with instruction,
He is pulling wires, moving
The shiny surfaces he depends on.
In the pattern he starves the explosions.
He sinks into the silence, he turns
Through base leg onto breathless final,
The horizon tightening around him.

Slowly now he is hurrying
To where nothing supports him.
With perfect timing, at last
He is not flying successfully,
The enormous real tearing past him.
On the hardstand he rolls to a standstill.
Safe on the dangerous ground
He draws a deep breath
Of the thin air he disappears into.
The toy town looms above him.

OUR DAILY VISITOR

Up front it's *au courant*
At the top of its voice.
Permanently excited,
Boldly it faces us down,
Bullying our inattention.
Daily it believes something
Important has happened.
Perhaps the point is to console us.
The enormous plane crashes in a simple prose
Where we are always among the survivors.

Though deep inside it minds terribly,
Will not disguise its opinion,
Everywhere else it is cheerful,
Ceaselessly so. And instructive.
Every day it improves our marriages.
It knows what we need to know.
On Sunday a huge leisure
Opens before us. It has read
A few good books for us
Lately and tells us about them.
In broad outline it displays
Its sense of our humor.

In time we half believe in us,
This simple life. It informs us.
Day after day piles up in the basement
Where nothing can surprise us.
Every morning we awaken to this life.

THE TURING GAME

"Attacking the tedious question whether machines can think Turing proposed a game for three players. It differs from most games in that each of them is trying to do something different. One player is a machine; it is trying to pass itself off as a person. Another is a person, trying to make it clear that he *is* a person. The third is an observer, trying to decide which is which. All communication is by electric teletypewriter, with the observer in a separate room."

Hugh Kenner, *The Counterfeiters*,
pp. 109–10

Any damn fool or accurate machine,
Having a whole history on paper
Authority, can spout a name and birthdate.
In the game, to succeed you must fail.
To be believed, you must remember to forget
Things it seems impossible you cannot recall.
But this will come to you naturally.
Now if only you will add to your set
Or magazine of talkative, correct opinions
A confident unfaith in what is true,
You are the man, that mistaken animal,
And for once this works to your advantage,
Invincible ignorance sweeping you to victory.

Should you be in fact the machine
You will find that you too are equipped
With the ruins of an education.
Briskly you fail to distinguish precisely
Latitude and longitude, Jacobite and Jacobin.
A graceless prose, too, will have been provided.
Now having ensured your inaccuracy,
As a last touch the Programmer,
That novelist, must make you vain,
Issuing you an unimportant secret

Defect you will take endless pains
Always to conceal. Thus he perfects you:
An ashamed machine may deceive the Observer

Who is, as we are told, human.
But suppose you really are the man
You think you are. Then you abide his question,
Confident he will expose you at last.
Though of course you both may be mistaken.
Because he is human he may never ask
You what you think
Like a clock at three in the morning
Or why you have buried you
Somewhere you can never look. You pray
He panics you with such questions.
You could not tell him these things and thus
He would discover you, that truth.

Whichever you are you await the decision.
As if you hoped you were that wrong
At heart, that chattering, stammering animal,
You keep taking every care to act natural.
As if you thought that might deceive some observer.

THE ALTERATIONS

This is the superior shop,
This glimmering long room
Where they will make you a man.
They will turn you out one
Properly, some regiment
Dangling at the collar.

Stitch by stitch every size
They assemble by hand
In their own workrooms.
Rank after rank the sober array
Of 40-Regulars
Is drawn up for your inspection.

Although you take your time
Choosing among all this subtle distinction,
Something is wrong with the hang of the thing.
This perfection will not sit
To the wry neck and dropping shoulder.
These it falls to the fitter to alter.

Sharply his chalk defines
How you depart from the pattern.
He confides to his book
Each fault of conformation.
On breast and scapula
He designs a bold distortion.

In the workroom someone must undo
What someone did well. Stitch by stitch
He resembles it to your imperfection.
Now it is properly yours.
In disguise you square your shoulders.
It becomes you, this deformation.

A PARTICULAR CHILD

Even in the expert books
No one quite understands him,
A darkness that gathers in the corner.

Or in the top of the house he rages.
Every hand is against him.
Though he too will never grow
To understand him,
Though he is beyond him,
In the distance every day
He is increasing. *He will do such things*!
What they are he does not know
But they shall be. . . ! They will preserve him.

Day after day he is falling,
The darkness that covers him.
Every evening the table is laid before him
In the presence of his enemies.
The terrors of the earth surround him.

THE CURE

People are insensitive. Unkind.
The Funny Farm, they call it,
The Laughing Academy.
Well, you did not find it amusing.
At all. Sometimes it was . . .
Well, whatever it was . . . boring?
A desolation. In the swell hotel
Fallen on evil days in the mountains
You have no words for what they do
To you on schedule first thing in the morning.

Now you are an empty bed, a vacancy.
Someone will have to pay for this.
You are coming down from the mountain
At last, a word burning on your lips.
They have made a desert and they call it peace.
Wherever you go you are going
To leave behind you that desolation.

BOXTRAP

It's child's play, this dead end
Anyone can add to nature—
A couple of feet of darkness
You knock together in the basement.

The rabbit's chance is his
Talent for suspicion.
A deliciousness? In these woods?
He is hungry, he is
Not a rational animal.
He enters this invention.

It is humane
If you remember to vent it.
Nothing tears, is broken.
He may live for days
In the dark on your temptation.

Twice a week
With your bare hands
You visit it,
This simple engine.
In the moral box
The bait is taken,
This square meal
You have built
Yourself in the basement.

911

A wailing over the houses.
                              Suddenly the day
Has turned serious for someone—
A date he has survived
Carelessly for years, the anniversary of nothing.
Now this is the day he must keep if he can.
In the middle of a mild March morning
In his own house the clock has struck at him.

On the street among our errands
We are glad he is being driven
At speed out of our Saturday.
Though we know he is no one we know,
He is our thought that we can hardly bear.
We stare him out of our lives.
Or we avert our eyes
As from the spectacle of great failure.

THE VISITING HOURS

Impossible. Nobody's home here
Under the coat-tree of apparatus.
Though every day we bring them
Our duty to them,
They are not there
To be visited, these animated
Imitations of their life.

Because they have lived their life
They are not here to be visited
But to receive correction.
Our gossip now insipid
As the glass of water beside them,
They gripe like soldiers in their disciplines.
Because they have lived their life
They down their salutary poisons.

Soon they will be delivered from their
Incarceration, taking a kind of wing.
Dear God, I say,
I shall come to this.
Thus shall I be visited.
The hours convey this instruction.
I lie in every bed
Where they are learning how
We learn to live without them.

ON THE LIST

As Who Isn't? his snobbery protests.
Still, he is pleased to be included.
As if his daily imitation
Of one of the grownups had succeeded,
Here he is among the real
Doctors and other serious persons.
Now he is somebody at last,
And there is his full name to prove it.
And an occupation. Out of the wide
Range of narrow choices the proprietors
Of the list provided he elected one.
He appears in print to be an Educator.

Most of the rest the proprietors
Left entirely to him.
Here he may be born when he chooses
And no one will correct him,
Certainly not his curtly acknowledged parents.
Now he may have as few wives as he wanted.
For a couple of lines his schooling goes smoothly.
Then he begins to rise in his profession,
Arriving at last at his home
Or office address and telephone number.

Every couple of years they ask him again
Who he is. He adds a child, a line
Of honors and awards, the grants
That prove he is a formidable beggar.
Yet it goes without saying that much
Must go unsaid. One principle
Ruling these little lives is omission.
Even the proprietors do not pretend
To offer anything like a full account.
Think how many things there is no room for.
Here everyone is friendless and unbrothered.
And where shall he record his treasured losses?

Someday when they ask their question
He will not be able to return an answer.
Then the proprietors must
Edit him out of the list.
By name. The object of an intention.
Perhaps this confers some distinction:
One dies and has to leave the foolish pages.
As if some purpose had been served at last.
But for now he is one inch tall
Including all his publications,
And he is a little proud of that.
Although he knows it comes to nothing much,
Bound in the color of blood
He soldiers on among his gray companions—
He and all these strangers by the thousand.

TO THOSE WHO SHARE
MY BIRTHDAY   6.18.31.

It is ours alone, this day,
Ours alone in our thousands.
By dozens the million
We love gather
In private celebration.

And always we record it,
This day special to us.
As shadow the happiness returns,
Every one of us
The center of that picture.

Some few of us will die
This day we all set out on.
They will leave us this day,
The circle closing
With idiot perfection.

Strangers, every day
We die, we leave us,
We leave us strangers.
How few we will become,
Alone in all our houses!

Let the engraving light
Record us, strangers—
As always it recorded
Us this happy day,
The past promising before us.

THE UNBURIED

for M.M.Z.

My dear, who are they years ago
By that weedy river? He has lost
Something and she
Is helping him to find it.

They are only a day
Old together. They do not know
The river flows. The time
They will have lost
Closes about them.

Look! It shines before them,
What they are looking for.
This is taking years.
If only we could guide them!

No. Though we know who they are
Who are wandering there,
The dangerous years
Ago rising about them,

We know we must leave them alone.
For a time thus shall we protect them:
For a time they are wandering there,
Though they are lost to us,
Us who are lost to us,
Lost in recollection.

THE GOOD TOURISTS

Everything these two see is recommended.
Though they may not know a dolmen from a corbel,
Taking their studious improving pleasure
They open the book to the place before them.
"Note the amazing medieval brickwork." Or
"To your left you are likely to see sheep grazing."
They lift their eyes from the page and they do.
Obedient for weeks they climb the stile
And turn at the fingerpost's direction. Always they ask
Permission of the owner and keep to the footpath,
Leaving no trash or other trace behind them.

And always they pause at the miraculous view.
It is not clear what they are looking for
In the meticulous distance, what they pick out
As if picked out in tapestry before them.
Time at its famous crewel-work again?
Wherever they go they shall not be disappointed.
At evening they trail home across the landscape
They were promised in the book, the ruins
Having closed at six and the light failing.
Though they will leave no trace behind them,
Morning after morning they will rise
Again to gaze on what is set before them.

A WORD FROM THE EXAMINERS

What we here require of you is
That you repeat a little history tidily.
One glance at the paper
And all around you a couple of dozen
Steel traps snap at the first question.
Only you only stare at what lies before you.
You cannot remember what you have to say
In your own words we have given you.

But suddenly what door flies open? You see
Our way before you. Now you are a headful
Of sober fact in noonday illumination.
For an hour now you can assign each tree
Its place in the forest, things you did not know
You knew pouring out like a confession.

This is a kind of forgetting
It all into the absorbing paper.
One by one the early finishers drift away.
Empty-headed you arise
From the sleep of concentration.
In black and white the hour is on the wall.
Now you must leave the past behind you.
Though you hope you have composed
Some sort of explanation
Of the events we hold you responsible for,
At the end you write *Time!* because there is none.

READING MYSELF ASLEEP

I have willed these ends—
The unaffecting dead,
Their throats cut in the cozy villages
Where I could never live.
I am reading myself asleep.
Every evening I require
These occasions of oblivion.

Here where women know best
Or the alien, step-by-step Inspector,
Beyond my wildest surmises the mild
Surprises I am offered take me in.
Page by page I attend
The innocent to their dismission.
Under my right hand the work diminishes.
I am reading myself asleep.
The patient dead await their explanation.
From the first all this was beginning to end.

THE COUNTRY BEYOND THE HILL

Without warning you come to the unremarkable
Rise in the land that hides it—the place
You have never visited, familiar as home.
The Country Beyond the Hill—it spells
Itself to you in these capitals.
You turn a panicky back on it.

You have seen what cannot be seen
From here: how while you do not visit there
A two-lane road is winding
Down to the village square.
The Presbyterian clock is striking.
While you stay away the dentist
Over the bank is drilling
Someone's tooth forever for an instant
And for years a hurrying
Adulterer enters the breathless partner.
A cloud is stuck in a corner
Of the air and, like everyone
Else, everyone supposes
This is the present only for a moment.

This is years from now
While you do not visit it.
At last you will come
To it from another quarter. Every road
Will lead you there.
Without warning, it will surround you—
The only place to make you welcome.
You will lift your eyes
To the hill beyond this country.
Now the clock begins to finish striking.
Now it is years from now at last.
This is where you are going to live forever.

THE CLUB OF THE ONLY CHILDREN

We are all great readers here and began early.
In the Library we muse over our huge collection
Of *The Princess and Curdie*. In her every edition
Alice lines the stairs up to the nursery
Under the eaves from which you may look down
Each into his own secret garden
(Which, after your tea, you will wish to explore).

Or so I believe. For the other members
The books may not be as I have named them.
(Here is one for you. Perhaps when it is opened
A ship will sail away from a great wailing
Forever toward the horizon, toward the island.
There you will step ashore, and in the illustration
The black sails will come up out of the dunnage.)

But for my part, and speaking for myself alone,
I say we are happy here. We have ourselves
And no one disturbs you. For company
Open the book. Goodbye. I bid you welcome.

JOHN N. MORRIS

John N. Morris was educated at the Augusta Military Academy, Hamilton College, and Columbia University. At present he teaches eighteenth-century English literature at Washington University in St. Louis. The recipient of a Guggenheim Fellowship and an Award in Letters from the Academy and Institute of Arts and Letters, he is the author of a critical study, VERSIONS OF THE SELF: STUDIES IN ENGLISH AUTOBIOGRAPHY (1966), *and of three earlier books of poems,* GREEN BUSINESS (1970), THE LIFE BESIDE THIS ONE (1975) *and* THE GLASS HOUSES (1980).